The First Stamp: Dad's Old Stamp

Adam had always seen his dad carefully sorting through a large album filled with small, colorful pieces of paper. Adam didn't know much about them, but he could see they meant a lot to his dad. One day, as his dad sat down to look through his collection, Adam's curiosity got the best of him.

"Dad," Adam asked, peering over his dad's shoulder, "what are all these little papers?"

His dad chuckled. "These aren't just little pieces of paper, Adam. These are stamps, and they're like tiny windows to different parts of history and the world. Each one tells a story."

Intrigued, Adam asked, "Can you tell me about them?"

His dad smiled and nodded, flipping carefully to a special page. "This is the very first stamp I ever collected," he said, pointing to a small, slightly faded stamp in the corner of the page. The stamp showed a picture of an old sailing ship, with a date from many years ago. Adam's eyes widened.

"This stamp is called *The Seafarer,*" his dad explained. "When I was your age, my father—your grandpa—gave it to me as a gift. He told me this was a special stamp because it came from his favorite collection. This ship," he continued, pointing to the image, "represents a time when people used boats to send messages across the sea."

Adam imagined a time long ago, with sailors delivering messages from one country to another. It seemed like a magical journey. "Wow, Dad! So, stamps are like little pieces of history?"

"Yes," his dad replied. "Each stamp can tell us about something unique, whether it's a famous event, a historic figure, or an interesting place."

Adam felt inspired and wanted to know more. "How did you get other stamps? Did Grandpa give them all to you?"

"Not all of them," his dad said, chuckling. "Over the years, I started collecting them myself. Some I found at the post office, others I traded with friends who also collected stamps. Every time I added a new one, it felt like finding a new treasure."

Adam took a closer look at *The Seafarer* and noticed tiny details he hadn't seen before: the sails on the ship, the waves beneath it, and even a small date in the corner. He was fascinated by how much detail could fit onto something so small.

"Dad," Adam said excitedly, "do you think I could start my own collection too?"

His dad's eyes sparkled with excitement. "Of course! I'd love to help you. We can find some stamps together, maybe even some from different countries."

Adam beamed, imagining himself finding tiny treasures from around the world, just like his dad had. "Can I start with *The Seafarer*?" he asked.

His dad hesitated, then laughed, "Well, *The Seafarer* is very special to me, but you can have your own 'first stamp.' Let's see what we can find together. And who knows? Someday you might even find one as special as this."

That evening, they sat together, flipping through the album, and his dad shared stories about other stamps he had collected over the years. Each one had its own adventure, and Adam could hardly wait to start his own. For Adam, that evening marked the beginning of a journey into the fascinating world of stamp collecting, where history, stories, and cultures could all be discovered, one tiny stamp

Adam and the History of Stamps

The day after learning about his dad's first stamp, Adam couldn't stop thinking about stamps and their stories. He realized that these tiny bits of paper held pieces of history from all over the world. That morning, he eagerly asked his dad, "Can you tell me more about stamps and where they came from?"

His dad smiled and sat Adam down, ready to share the origins of stamps. "Well, Adam, the story of stamps begins almost two hundred years ago," he explained. "Before stamps existed, sending a letter was complicated. If someone wanted to mail a letter, the person receiving it had to pay for it, and it could be quite expensive!"

Adam was surprised. "So, if people didn't have money to pay for the letter, they couldn't get it?"

"Exactly," his dad replied. "Because of this, many letters went undelivered. It was a real problem. But then, a British teacher named Sir Rowland Hill had an idea that changed everything. In 1840, he created the first-ever postage stamp, called the *Penny Black.*"

Adam leaned forward, fascinated. "What did it look like?"

His dad reached into his collection, pulled out a small image of a black stamp, and handed it to Adam. "This is a replica of the *Penny Black.* It featured the profile of Queen Victoria, the queen of England at the time. People could buy the stamp for just one penny, stick it on their letter, and send it anywhere in England. The cost was covered by the sender, making it affordable for everyone."

Adam studied the small black stamp, marveling at its simple but elegant design. "So, this was the first stamp ever? That's amazing!"

"Yes," his dad said. "The *Penny Black* was so successful that other countries soon started creating their own stamps. By the late 1800s, stamps had spread worldwide. Each country began designing stamps that represented their unique cultures, historical figures, and landmarks."

Adam's eyes sparkled with excitement. "Wow, so stamps are like a piece of each country's story?"

"Exactly," his dad nodded. "Each one is a little glimpse into that country's identity. Some countries show their famous buildings, others show animals or flowers, and some even celebrate important events and people from their history."

Inspired, Adam asked, "Do we have any stamps from other countries in our collection?"

His dad smiled. "Yes, we do. Let me show you a few." He opened a page in his album filled with stamps from different countries. There was a stamp from Japan with cherry blossoms, one from Egypt with the Great Pyramids, and another from Brazil featuring a rainforest bird.

"Look at this one," his dad said, pointing to a stamp with a snowy mountain and a bear.

"This is from Canada, and it shows some of the country's wildlife and landscape."

Adam gazed at the stamps, each more beautiful and unique than the last. He felt like he was traveling around the world just by looking at them. "Dad, can I keep one of these?"

His dad laughed and shook his head. "Not yet, buddy! But if you start your own collection, I'll help you find your own stamps from different countries."

Adam's heart leapt with excitement. He could already picture himself with an album filled with stamps from all over the world, each one a piece of history and adventure. Collecting stamps, he realized, was like gathering pieces of the world to hold in his hands.

A Journey Around the World Through Stamps

Adam's curiosity about stamps was growing, and he was eager to learn more about the places and stories they represented. That evening, he sat down with his dad, who brought out a page filled with stamps from all corners of the globe. Each one had its own design, colors, and images, showing glimpses of faraway places.

"Dad," Adam asked, "can you tell me about some of these countries? I feel like each stamp is a little passport to somewhere new."

His dad smiled, thrilled by Adam's enthusiasm. "That's exactly right, Adam! Each of these stamps comes from a different country, showing what's special about that place. Some celebrate nature, others focus on culture, and some even show famous events or people."

Adam looked closely at a small green stamp with a tiny elephant on it. "Where's this one from?"

"That's from India," his dad explained. "The elephant is a symbol of wisdom and strength there. This stamp also shows India's appreciation for its natural wildlife. In fact, India has many national parks dedicated to protecting animals like elephants and tigers."

Adam imagined colorful markets, spicy scents, and jungles filled with elephants and tigers. "India sounds amazing!"

Next, his eyes landed on a bright yellow stamp with a castle perched on a mountain. "What about this one?"

His dad smiled. "That's from Germany, and the castle on the stamp is called Neuschwanstein Castle. It's one of the most famous castles in the world, and it looks like something from a fairytale! Germany is known for its castles, forests, and history."

Adam's mind filled with images of knights, ancient castles, and green forests. "Do people still live in castles there?"

His dad chuckled. "Not so much anymore, but they're important landmarks that show what life was like in the past."

Adam's attention then shifted to a blue stamp with an ocean wave and a dolphin leaping out of the water. "This one must be from somewhere near the ocean, right?"

"Good guess!" his dad replied. "That stamp is from Australia. Australia is famous for its beaches, coral reefs, and unique wildlife, like kangaroos and koalas. It's a place where the sea and the land are equally amazing."

Adam imagined swimming in clear blue waters, surrounded by dolphins and colorful fish. "I want to visit Australia one day!"

His dad nodded. "Collecting stamps is a great way to learn about places you might want to visit someday. It's like having a little piece of each country in your hands."

Then, Adam spotted a red stamp with a dragon on it. "What about this one? Is it from a place with dragons?"

His dad laughed, enjoying Adam's questions. "This is from China. The dragon is a powerful symbol there, representing strength and good fortune. Chinese culture is rich with symbols and legends, and the dragon is one of the most popular ones. Some festivals even have dragon dances to celebrate."

Adam could almost picture the vibrant celebrations, with dancers moving like dragons in the streets. He was amazed by how each stamp opened a window to a new world, each more exciting and colorful than the last.

After a while, Adam looked at his dad, his eyes bright with excitement. "Dad, stamps are like little adventures. I want to collect stamps from every country in the world!"

His dad smiled proudly. "That sounds like a wonderful goal, Adam. Each time you add a stamp to your collection, you'll be learning about a new place, its people, and its stories."

As they looked through the album, Adam felt like he was already traveling the world. For the first time, he realized how much there was to learn and explore just by looking at these tiny stamps, each one a little passport to a world of wonder and discovery.

The Stamp Album: A Treasure of Memories

Adam was now truly fascinated by stamps and the stories they held. He decided he wanted his own album to collect these tiny treasures from around the world. So, one sunny afternoon, he asked his dad, "Can we get an album for my stamp collection?"

His dad smiled, delighted by Adam's enthusiasm. "Of course, Adam! I remember the excitement of getting my first album. Let's make sure yours is special too." They set off to a local store that sold albums and collecting supplies, and Adam's excitement grew with every step.

When they reached the store, they found a section filled with albums in different colors, sizes, and designs. Adam's eyes lit up as he looked around, trying to choose the perfect one. He finally spotted a deep blue album with golden edges and a little compass on the cover. It looked like a treasure book waiting to be filled.

"Dad, this one! It looks like a book of adventures!" Adam exclaimed.

His dad agreed, "Great choice, Adam. This album will hold many memories and stories, just like mine. Now, let's get some stamp sheets so you can safely keep your stamps inside."

Once they returned home, Adam carefully opened his new album, admiring its empty pages, which he was eager to fill. His dad brought out a few stamps to help him get started: a stamp from Italy with a picture of the Leaning Tower of Pisa, one from Egypt with the pyramids, and another from Japan with cherry blossoms.

As Adam gently placed each stamp into the album, he realized that every stamp marked a memory. "Dad, do you remember when you got your first stamp?" he asked.

His dad nodded, reminiscing. "Yes, Adam, I was about your age. My dad, your grandpa, gave me a stamp from Brazil. I remember looking at the picture of the Amazon rainforest on it, with all its trees and birds. It was like holding a piece of the world in my hands."

Adam felt a new appreciation for his album. He wasn't just collecting stamps; he was collecting memories and stories, just like his dad had done. Each page felt like a chapter waiting to be filled with exciting discoveries.

Adam's dad then suggested, "You know, Adam, we could write little notes next to each stamp, saying where it's from and a special fact about it. That way, when you look back at your album, you'll remember not just the stamps, but also what you learned."

Adam loved the idea. With his dad's help, he wrote under the Italian stamp, *"Leaning Tower of Pisa, Italy: A tower famous for leaning to one side due to its soft foundation."* Next to the Egyptian stamp, he wrote, *"The Great Pyramids, Egypt: Ancient tombs built thousands of years ago."*

They spent the rest of the afternoon filling his album with stamps and stories. His dad even shared stories about some of the stamps he had collected over the years. Adam listened eagerly, feeling like each stamp was a piece of treasure, a memory shared between him and his dad.

As the sun began to set, Adam looked at his album with pride. He had only a few stamps, but he could already see the beginning of something wonderful. It wasn't just an album; it was a book of adventures, memories, and dreams of all the places he would explore through his collection.

"Thank you, Dad," Adam said softly, hugging his album. "This is the best treasure ever."

His dad ruffled his hair and smiled. "Remember, Adam, it's not just about having stamps. It's about the stories they hold and the memories we make together."

Adam nodded, realizing he'd found something more precious than just stamps. He'd found a way to connect with his dad and the world, one tiny treasure at a time.

Adam Discovers Rare Stamps

Adam's stamp collection was growing, and each day he felt more and more connected to the stories these tiny pieces of paper held. One afternoon, while organizing his album, his dad came over with a glint of excitement in his eye. "Adam, would you like to learn about rare stamps today?"

Adam's eyes widened with curiosity. "Rare stamps? Are they different from the ones I have?"

His dad nodded. "Yes, rare stamps are special because they are either very old, have a unique story, or were printed in limited numbers. Collectors treasure these stamps because each one has a fascinating history."

Adam felt a thrill run through him. "Do we have any rare stamps in our collection?"

Smiling, his dad opened an old, worn-out album from his own collection and carefully turned to a page near the middle. He pointed to a small, slightly faded stamp with a picture of a plane on it. "This stamp is called *The Inverted Jenny,*" his dad explained. "It's one of the most famous rare stamps in the world because of a mistake. The plane on it was printed upside-down by accident, which made it very valuable to collectors."

Adam's jaw dropped. "A mistake made it special?"

"Yes!" his dad laughed. "Sometimes, mistakes can make things unique. Only a few of these stamps exist because they were quickly corrected, so each one is now very valuable."

Adam studied *The Inverted Jenny* carefully. It seemed almost magical that a simple printing error could make a stamp so special. "That's amazing, Dad! Do we have any more rare stamps?"

His dad nodded, flipping to another page. This time, he showed Adam a stamp from

Sweden. It was bright yellow and very old-looking. "This one is called *The Treskilling Yellow.* It's famous because it was supposed to be printed in green, but some copies came out yellow by mistake. Only one of these stamps is known to exist today."

Adam couldn't believe it. "Only one in the whole world?"

"That's right," his dad replied, smiling. "And that's what makes it so valuable. Rare stamps are like little treasures hidden around the world, each with its own mystery."

Adam felt a surge of excitement. "I want to find a rare stamp one day! Do you think I could?"

His dad chuckled. "You never know, Adam. Some collectors spend years looking, while others find rare stamps by sheer luck. The fun part is in the journey of discovering and learning, just like we are now."

Adam thought about all the stamps in his collection and wondered if any of them held hidden secrets. He realized that rare stamps weren't just about money or fame; they were pieces of history, accidents, and mysteries waiting to be uncovered.

After looking at a few more famous rare stamps, Adam felt inspired. He decided he would keep his eyes open for any stamp that seemed different or unusual, and he'd ask his dad to help him research its history. Perhaps one day, he'd find his own rare stamp, a treasure that would add a special story to his collection.

As they closed the album, Adam's dad said, "Remember, Adam, it's not just about rare stamps. Every stamp you collect has a story worth learning. And who knows, maybe one day you'll have a story about a rare stamp you discovered on your own."

Adam nodded, his eyes bright with excitement and determination. Collecting stamps was more than just a hobby now; it was a journey into a world of mystery and adventure. And as he looked at his own album, he wondered what secrets his collection might one day hold.

The Quest for the King's Stamp

Adam's collection was growing beautifully, and he was proud of each stamp he'd collected so far. But after learning about rare stamps, Adam couldn't stop thinking about finding a stamp with its own fascinating story. One day, his dad noticed his excitement and said, "Adam, would you like to go on a quest for a special stamp today?"

Adam's eyes lit up. "A quest? What kind of stamp are we looking for?"

His dad leaned closer, lowering his voice as if sharing a secret. "Today, we're looking for something called *The King's Stamp.* It's not a rare stamp exactly, but it's one of my favorites because of the history behind it. It was issued by a small country in Europe and has a picture of the country's beloved king."

Adam was instantly intrigued. "A stamp with a king on it? Where can we find it?"

His dad smiled. "We're going to a special shop in town where collectors often trade stamps. The owner there has stamps from all over the world. Who knows, maybe we'll find *The King's Stamp* or even discover another hidden treasure."

They set off together, and Adam's heart raced with excitement as they reached the shop. Inside, the shop was like a treasure trove, with shelves and cases filled with albums and individual stamps, all neatly displayed. Adam could hardly believe his eyes as he scanned the stamps: animals, buildings, famous people, flowers, and even old ships.

"Welcome!" the shop owner greeted them warmly. "Are you looking for anything specific today?"

Adam looked up at his dad, who nodded for him to speak. "I'm looking for a stamp called *The King's Stamp,*" Adam said, trying to sound confident.

The owner smiled knowingly. "Ah, a fine choice. That stamp was issued by the country of Liechtenstein many years ago. It has a portrait of King Franz Josef II, a much-loved ruler from a small but beautiful country."

Adam was thrilled. "Do you have one here?"

The owner thought for a moment, then guided them to a glass case filled with special stamps. He pointed to a carefully preserved stamp with the portrait of a king wearing a royal uniform. The stamp was simple yet elegant, with the king's face framed in a classic border.

Adam's dad looked at him and asked, "What do you think, Adam? Is this the kind of stamp you want to add to your collection?"

Adam's eyes sparkled. "Yes, it's perfect! It feels like a stamp with a real story behind it."

The shop owner nodded in agreement. "King Franz Josef II was known for being a kind and wise leader. Many people in Liechtenstein admired him, and that's why his stamp became so popular. Collectors appreciate it because it reminds us of a good king from a small country that values its history and traditions."

Adam carefully took the stamp in his hands, feeling like he was holding a piece of history. "Thank you," he said to the shop owner. "I'm really excited to add *The King's Stamp* to my collection."

After purchasing the stamp, Adam and his dad walked home, where Adam placed it proudly in his album. He wrote a little note beneath it, just as they'd done with his other stamps: *"The King's Stamp from Liechtenstein: King Franz Josef II, a beloved leader from a tiny European country."*

As he closed his album, Adam felt a sense of accomplishment. He hadn't just collected another stamp; he had gone on a quest, learned about a king, and discovered a piece of history. He knew that every time he looked at *The King's Stamp,* he'd remember this special adventure with his dad.

And as he drifted off to sleep that night, Adam dreamed of more quests for stamps with stories waiting to be uncovered. His collection was becoming not just a hobby but a journey, one filled with history, adventure, and endless discovery.

How Stamps are Made: A Story from the Printing Press

One rainy afternoon, Adam was flipping through his album when he started to wonder about something he'd never thought of before. "Dad," he asked, "how are stamps made? They're so tiny, but they have so many details!"

His dad chuckled and replied, "That's a great question, Adam! Making stamps is actually an art. Each stamp is designed carefully, and it goes through several steps before it's ready to be collected. Would you like to visit a printing press to see how it's done?"

Adam's eyes sparkled with excitement. "Yes! I'd love that!"

The next day, Adam and his dad visited a printing press that occasionally gave tours to curious visitors. As they entered, Adam could smell the faint scent of ink and hear the humming of the large machines. A friendly guide greeted them, ready to explain the fascinating world of stamp production.

"Welcome!" the guide said. "Today, we'll take you on a journey through the steps of making a stamp. Every stamp starts as a design. Artists work on tiny sketches, deciding what colors, shapes, and details will go into each stamp. They want to make sure each stamp tells a story and represents something special."

Adam was amazed. "So, someone actually draws every stamp?"

The guide nodded. "Exactly. Once the artist finishes the design, it's transferred onto a special plate, which is used for printing. The printing plates are like giant stamps themselves, but they're covered in tiny grooves to hold the ink."

They moved to the printing area, where Adam saw large sheets of blank paper going through a huge machine. As the sheets passed through, they came out covered in rows of colorful stamps, each perfectly detailed.

"After the printing, each sheet is carefully checked," the guide explained. "Workers look for any mistakes, making sure each stamp is just right. Only perfect stamps go on to the next step."

Adam leaned closer to see the sheets, noticing how detailed and vivid each little stamp was. "What happens to the ones that aren't perfect?" he asked.

"They're set aside and recycled," the guide replied. "Collectors value stamps without any flaws, so it's important to make sure each one is as close to perfect as possible."

The guide then showed them the final step: perforation. A machine punched tiny holes between each stamp so they could be easily torn apart. "This is what gives stamps their unique edges," the guide said. "Once the perforation is done, the stamps are ready to be cut, packaged, and sent to post offices all over the country."

Adam was fascinated by the entire process. "Wow, so much work goes into each stamp! I never knew they were made so carefully."

The guide smiled, pleased with Adam's enthusiasm. "Yes, every stamp is a result of hard work and attention to detail. That's why collectors treasure them. They aren't just tiny pieces of paper; they're works of art."

After the tour, Adam and his dad thanked the guide and left the printing press. Adam felt like he had just discovered a new layer to his favorite hobby. That evening, as he looked at his album, he saw each stamp differently, appreciating the hard work that went into making each one special.

He looked at his dad and said, "I think I love stamps even more now, knowing how much effort goes into making them."

His dad nodded, smiling proudly. "It's amazing, isn't it? Collecting stamps means appreciating the art, the history, and now, even the process behind each one."

Adam hugged his album tightly, feeling grateful for the chance to learn about the journey each stamp took before it reached his collection. He knew that from then on, each new stamp would be more than just a piece of his collection; it would be a little masterpiece, crafted with care and skill.

Adam and the Holiday Stamps Collection

As the holiday season approached, Adam noticed colorful, festive stamps appearing on the mail that came to their home. Each one seemed brighter and more cheerful than the usual stamps, and they often featured snowflakes, ornaments, or winter scenes. Intrigued, Adam asked his dad, "Why do some stamps look so festive around this time of year?"

His dad chuckled. "Those are holiday stamps, Adam. Many countries create special stamps for the holiday season. They're only available for a limited time each year, making them very special for collectors."

Adam's eyes sparkled with excitement. "Can we collect some holiday stamps for our album?"

His dad smiled and nodded. "Of course! In fact, holiday stamps are a wonderful way to capture the spirit of each season. Some collectors only collect holiday-themed stamps because they come in so many unique designs."

The very next day, Adam and his dad visited the local post office to see what holiday stamps were available. As they arrived, they saw a display showcasing this year's holiday stamps: one had a cozy cabin in the snow, another showed children building a snowman, and a third had a bright, twinkling star. Adam loved each design and felt like each stamp carried its own festive story.

"Can we get them all, Dad?" he asked eagerly.

His dad agreed, and they purchased a small sheet of each design. Adam couldn't wait to add them to his album. When they got home, they carefully cut each stamp from the sheet and placed them on a special page he'd designated for holiday stamps.

As they arranged the stamps, his dad shared a fun fact. "Did you know, Adam, that holiday stamps are popular all around the world? Each country creates its own designs based on its holiday traditions. For example, in some places, you'll see stamps with Christmas trees and snowflakes, while other countries might show scenes from Hanukkah, Diwali, or even New Year celebrations."

Adam thought that was amazing. "So, holiday stamps aren't just about Christmas. They can celebrate all kinds of holidays?"

"Exactly," his dad replied. "Some collectors even try to gather holiday stamps from different countries to see how each place celebrates in its own way."

That gave Adam a great idea. "Maybe we could collect holiday stamps from around the world! We could learn about other countries' traditions as we go."

His dad beamed. "That's a fantastic idea, Adam. Collecting holiday stamps from different countries could help us explore the traditions, foods, and celebrations that make each culture unique."

They began their new quest for holiday stamps by reaching out to friends and family who lived in other countries, asking if they could send them any holiday stamps from their local post offices. Before long, envelopes began arriving with cheerful stamps from places Adam had never even dreamed of visiting. He received stamps with poinsettias from Mexico, lanterns from China, and even a colorful rangoli design from India.

Adam carefully added each new stamp to his album, writing a small note next to each one about its origin and the holiday it represented. His holiday stamp page soon became a collection of colors, designs, and stories from all around the world, each stamp a reminder of the different ways people celebrated the season.

One evening, as Adam looked over his holiday stamps, he felt a warmth and happiness that matched the spirit of the season. His album was no longer just a collection of stamps; it was a celebration of holiday cheer from every corner of the globe.

"Dad," he said, "this is my favorite page in the album. Each stamp feels like a gift from a different place."

His dad gave him a proud smile. "That's the beauty of holiday stamps, Adam. They remind us that no matter where we come from, everyone loves to celebrate. It brings people together, even if they're far apart."

Adam couldn't agree more. His holiday stamps were more than just pieces of paper; they were tokens of joy, culture, and connection. And each year, he looked forward to adding new stamps to his growing collection, knowing that with every stamp, he was holding a piece of the world's holiday spirit in his hands.

The Commemorative Stamp: A Story of Historic Moments

One day, while flipping through his album, Adam noticed a stamp with a unique design that stood out among the others. It featured a group of people waving flags, fireworks in the sky, and a large date printed boldly across the bottom. Curious, he turned to his dad and asked, "What's special about this stamp? It looks like it's celebrating something."

His dad smiled, recognizing the stamp. "That's a commemorative stamp, Adam. These stamps are made to honor special events, important people, or historic moments. They're like little reminders of big events, celebrating something that has meaning for many people."

Adam was fascinated. "So, this stamp tells a story about something that happened in the past?"

"Exactly," his dad replied. "This particular stamp was issued to celebrate the country's independence anniversary. It shows people celebrating together, symbolizing freedom and unity. It's a way of remembering a moment that changed history."

Adam looked closely at the stamp, appreciating the details that told a story. He saw children waving flags, fireworks lighting up the night sky, and families gathered together. "It's amazing how much they fit into such a small stamp!"

His dad nodded. "Commemorative stamps are special for that reason. They aren't just regular postage; they're carefully designed to honor something important. Sometimes, countries issue them to celebrate the end of a war, the founding of an important institution, or even the life of someone who made a big difference."

Adam was even more curious now. "Do we have other commemorative stamps in our collection?"

His dad took out a few more stamps, each one with its own unique design and story. There was a stamp celebrating the first moon landing, another honoring a famous scientist, and one that commemorated a historic peace treaty.

"This one," his dad said, pointing to the moon landing stamp, "was issued to celebrate the day humans first walked on the moon. Can you imagine? It was such an incredible achievement that they made a special stamp just to remember it."

Adam looked at the stamp in awe. "Wow, it's like a piece of history that people can hold in their hands."

"Exactly," his dad replied. "Commemorative stamps are like little souvenirs of these historic moments. People collect them because they're limited editions; they're only available for a short time, so having one is like owning a piece of history."

Inspired, Adam decided he wanted to create a special section in his album just for commemorative stamps. He carefully arranged the stamps his dad had shown him, placing the moon landing and independence stamps side by side. Then, he wrote small notes under each one, describing what they represented.

As they continued organizing, Adam thought of all the amazing things commemorative stamps could capture. "Do you think one day they'll make a commemorative stamp for something I'll be a part of, Dad?"

His dad smiled warmly. "You never know, Adam. Every great achievement starts with someone who dreams big and works hard. Maybe one day, you'll be part of something historic."

Adam felt a thrill at the thought. He imagined stamps featuring great moments of his own life, like his first big achievement or an adventure he hadn't yet taken. Collecting commemorative stamps was more than just a hobby; it was a way to hold onto the memories and milestones that shape history.

With each new commemorative stamp he added, Adam felt connected to the stories, people, and moments that had shaped the world. His album had become a time capsule of history, and he was excited to keep exploring, learning, and discovering new stories with every stamp he found.

Adam Collects Animal Stamps from Around the World

Adam's collection had become a mix of beautiful stamps, each with its own unique story. One day, as he was looking through his album, he noticed a small collection of stamps featuring animals. He saw a majestic lion from Africa, a panda from China, and a soaring eagle from the United States. This gave him an idea. "Dad," he said, "what if I collect stamps of animals from around the world? It would be like building my own zoo, but on paper!"

His dad chuckled, loving the idea. "That sounds like a fantastic project, Adam. Animals are popular on stamps because they represent the unique wildlife of each country. You could end up with a collection that teaches you about animals from every continent!"

Excited, Adam and his dad went to the local post office to search for animal stamps. The post office had a special display of stamps with different themes, and Adam's eyes immediately landed on a set of animal stamps featuring creatures from all over the globe. There was a kangaroo from Australia, a polar bear from Canada, and even a peacock from India.

"Can we get these, Dad?" Adam asked, pointing to the set. His dad nodded, and they bought the stamps to start his new animal-themed collection.

Back at home, Adam carefully added the new stamps to a page he'd dedicated just for animals. He placed each one neatly, admiring the diversity of animals that each stamp showcased. He was fascinated by how each stamp seemed to capture the beauty and essence of its animal.

As they added more stamps, Adam's dad suggested, "Why don't you write a little fact about each animal next to the stamp? That way, you'll learn more about them as you go."

Adam loved the idea. Next to the kangaroo, he wrote, *"Kangaroo: Found in Australia, they can jump over 9 meters in a single bound!"* By the polar bear, he noted, *"Polar Bear: Lives in the Arctic and has thick fur to stay warm in the freezing cold."*

Over the next few weeks, Adam's animal collection grew. Friends and family began sending him stamps from their travels, each with animals he'd never seen before. He received a beautiful stamp of a toucan from Brazil, a camel from Egypt, and a koala from Australia. Each one fascinated him, adding a new piece to his growing zoo of stamps.

One evening, as he looked over his collection, Adam felt proud. "Dad, look at all the animals! I feel like I'm visiting these places just by looking at the stamps."

His dad nodded. "That's the magic of stamps, Adam. They let you explore and learn about the world without leaving home. And with animals, you get to learn about the creatures that make each place special."

Adam felt inspired. "Do you think I could collect enough animal stamps to cover every continent?"

His dad grinned. "I think that's a wonderful goal! And it's definitely possible. Animals are such a popular theme that there are stamps featuring creatures from every part of the world. Just imagine having a complete collection—animals from the jungles of South America, the savannas of Africa, the forests of Asia, and even the icy lands of Antarctica!"

Adam beamed, already imagining his album filled with animals from every corner of the globe. Each new stamp would be an addition to his growing collection, a reminder of the diversity and beauty of nature. His animal stamps were more than just collectibles; they were windows into the natural wonders of the world.

From that day on, Adam's mission was clear. He would build the ultimate animal stamp collection, filling his album with creatures great and small. Each time he added a new stamp, he would learn a bit more about the animals and the places they called home, making his collection a true celebration of nature's incredible variety.

And as he added the latest stamp—a majestic lion from Kenya—Adam felt like an explorer on an adventure, discovering the world one animal stamp at a time.

The Mystery of the Missing Stamp

One sunny afternoon, Adam was organizing his album and admiring his growing collection when he noticed something unusual. One of his favorite stamps—a beautiful, brightly colored butterfly from Costa Rica—was missing! He had placed it in a special spot just a few days earlier, but now there was only an empty space where it should have been.

Adam frowned, puzzled. "Dad, my butterfly stamp is gone! I put it right here, but now it's missing."

His dad joined him, examining the album. "Are you sure you didn't move it to another page, Adam? Sometimes we rearrange things without noticing."

Adam shook his head. "No, I was saving that spot just for my butterfly stamps. I wanted to collect butterflies from different countries, and this was my first one."

His dad scratched his chin thoughtfully. "Well, if it's really missing, maybe we should investigate. Let's search around the room and see if it fell out of the album."

Adam agreed, and the two of them started a careful search. They looked under the table, behind the couch, and even checked

Adam's bookshelf. But there was no sign of the butterfly stamp. Adam was beginning to feel a bit sad. It wasn't just a stamp; it was a special part of his collection, one he was especially proud of.

Just then, Adam's younger sister, Lily, entered the room, holding something small and colorful in her hand. "Adam, look what I found!" she said, grinning proudly.

To Adam's surprise, she was holding the butterfly stamp! He quickly asked, "Lily, where did you find this?"

Lily looked a bit guilty. "I thought it was pretty, so I borrowed it to put in my book. I was going to give it back, but I forgot."

Adam felt a wave of relief and couldn't help but laugh. "Lily, stamps are special, and each one has its own place in my collection. If you'd like to look at them, you can always ask, and I'll show them to you."

Lily nodded, looking a little embarrassed. "I'm sorry, Adam. I didn't mean to take it without asking."

Adam's dad smiled, giving Lily a reassuring pat on the back. "It's okay, Lily. It's good that you like stamps too. Maybe one day you can start a collection of your own."

Adam thought about it and had an idea. "Lily, how about this? I'll help you start your own little stamp collection. We can look for stamps with flowers or animals, something you'd like. That way, you won't have to borrow mine!"

Lily's face lit up with excitement. "Really? I'd love that!"

Together, Adam and his dad helped Lily set up a small album, and they gave her a few starter stamps that Adam no longer needed. She was thrilled, carefully placing each one in her album with Adam's guidance.

Later that day, Adam placed his butterfly stamp back in its original spot, feeling grateful to have it back and happy that Lily was now a fellow stamp collector. His collection had taught him more than just history and geography—it had helped him share his passion with his sister and bring them closer together.

As they admired their albums side by side, Adam realized that the mystery of the missing stamp had turned into something much better: a new bond with his sister, and a shared love for collecting tiny pieces of the world.

Adam's First Stamp Trade

Adam's stamp collection had grown beautifully, with stamps from many countries and a range of themes. One day, while admiring his collection, he noticed

74

he had a few duplicate stamps—two extra stamps with the image of the Eiffel Tower from France and another pair showing the Great Wall of China. He remembered something his dad had once told him: "Collectors often trade stamps to get new ones they don't have."

Excited by the idea, Adam went to his dad and asked, "Dad, do you think I could trade some of my extra stamps to get new ones?"

His dad nodded, smiling. "That's a great idea, Adam! Trading is a big part of collecting. Many collectors swap duplicates to expand their collections. How about we go to a stamp trading event at the local library this weekend? You might find other collectors who'd love to trade with you."

On Saturday, they arrived at the library, which had a section set up for collectors of all ages. Tables were filled with albums, loose stamps, and small magnifying glasses for close examination. Adam was amazed by how many different stamps he saw, each one unique and special.

Nervously, Adam approached a boy around his age who was looking through his own album. "Hi, I'm Adam," he said. "Would you be interested in trading stamps?"

The boy smiled and introduced himself. "I'm Ben! Sure, I'd love to trade. Do you have any extras?"

Adam showed him the duplicates he had, and Ben's eyes lit up when he saw the Eiffel Tower stamp. "I've been looking for a France stamp! I have one from Brazil that shows the Amazon rainforest. Would you like to trade?"

Adam examined the Brazil stamp, amazed by its beautiful design of lush trees and exotic birds. It was unlike any stamp he had in his collection. "Yes, I'd love that!" he said, handing over one of his Eiffel Tower stamps in exchange for the rainforest one.

Ben carefully placed the Eiffel Tower stamp in his album, and Adam added the Amazon rainforest stamp to his own collection. It was his first trade, and he felt a thrill of excitement, knowing he'd exchanged a part of his collection to make it even more special.

Afterward, Adam met another collector, a girl named Sofia, who was interested in one of his Great Wall of China stamps. In return, she offered a beautiful stamp from Greece, featuring an ancient temple surrounded by olive branches. Adam happily made the trade, feeling as though he was traveling around the world, one stamp at a time.

By the end of the event, Adam had made a few new friends and collected several unique stamps from places he'd never even thought of before. As he and his dad walked home, he looked over his new stamps, each one a reminder of the friendly exchanges he'd made that day.

His dad smiled, watching Adam's excitement. "Trading is a wonderful way to build your collection, Adam. Not only do you get new stamps, but you also meet people who share the same interest and passion."

Adam nodded, feeling a new sense of connection to the collecting world. His collection wasn't just about finding stamps—it was about the friendships and stories behind each one. He couldn't wait for his next trading adventure, knowing there were still so many stamps—and stories—to discover.

That night, as he placed his new stamps in his album, Adam realized he had added more than just new designs to his collection; he had added memories, friendships, and a little piece of the world, shared with others who loved stamps just as much as he did.

Adam's Adventure with Animal Series Stamps

Adam was looking through his album when he noticed something interesting: he had a few stamps featuring animals, but they were from different series. One showed a tiger from India, another a bear from Russia, and a third a bald eagle from the United States. Inspired, Adam thought, "What if I try to collect a complete set of animal series stamps? That would be an incredible addition to my album!"

Adam shared his idea with his dad, who nodded enthusiastically. "That's a fantastic idea, Adam! Many countries release special series of stamps featuring their native animals. Collecting a full set would be a real achievement. How about we start by finding out which animal series are available at the post office?"

The next day, they visited the post office, where the clerk was happy to help Adam with his project. She showed them a collection featuring animals from Africa, with stamps of lions, elephants, zebras, and rhinos. Adam was thrilled. "These would be perfect for my collection!"

He bought a few of the stamps to start his animal series and carefully placed them in a special section of his album. As he did, he wrote little notes next to each one, learning more about each animal as he went. Next to the lion, he wrote, *"Lion: Known as the king of the jungle, lions live in prides and are found mostly in Africa."* For the elephant, he added, *"Elephant: The largest land animal, famous for its intelligence and strong family bonds."*

As he continued his search for more animal series, Adam learned about different habitats and ecosystems from all over the world. Soon he had stamps from the African savanna, the rainforests of South America, and the forests of Europe. Each set brought a new perspective, and his album began to look like a wildlife encyclopedia.

One day, his dad surprised him with a gift—a stamp set featuring underwater creatures! There was a dolphin, a sea turtle, and a colorful coral reef. Adam added them to his animal section and was fascinated by the diversity of marine life. He realized that his collection wasn't just about animals he could see on land; it was about discovering the incredible variety of life in every part of the world.

Adam's friends at school soon noticed his growing collection, and he decided to show them his animal series. They were amazed by the beautiful stamps and the stories behind each animal. One friend, Sam, pointed to the rainforest stamps and said, "This is so cool, Adam! It's like you have your own animal library!"

Adam beamed with pride, happy to share his collection. He realized that his album wasn't just for himself—it was something he could share with others, teaching them about the wonderful animals that lived in different places.

Eventually, Adam completed his first full series with the animals of Africa set. He looked over the stamps and felt a deep sense of accomplishment. Collecting each one had been a small adventure, a journey that connected him to the world's wildlife.

That night, as Adam added a final note to his animal series, he felt inspired. His collection had become a celebration of the natural world, one that he could continue to build and explore. And with each new series he collected, he knew he'd be adding not only to his album but to his understanding of the amazing creatures that shared the world with him.

Adam's Discovery of Miniature Sheet Stamps

Adam was browsing through a stamp magazine when something unusual caught his eye. It was a picture of a large, beautifully illustrated sheet that featured a collection of tiny stamps within it, all related to a single theme. Each stamp was connected, forming a miniature story on one page. "Wow, Dad! Look at this!" he exclaimed, pointing to the magazine. "What kind of stamps are these?"

His dad took a closer look and smiled. "Those are called miniature sheets, Adam. They're special sheets of stamps that are usually themed around one topic, like nature, space, or famous landmarks. Each sheet has a collection of stamps arranged to form a unique picture, almost like a small poster."

Adam's curiosity was piqued. "So, it's like a story in stamps?"

"Exactly," his dad replied. "Miniature sheets are popular among collectors because they're both stamps and a form of art. They're often created to celebrate something important, like an anniversary or a famous event. Each stamp in the sheet is unique, but together they tell a complete story."

Excited to see one up close, Adam and his dad headed to the post office to see if they could find a miniature sheet for his collection. The clerk was delighted to show them several sheets, each with a different theme. One featured ancient dinosaurs, with each stamp displaying a different species. Another had a space theme, with planets, stars, and astronauts. But the one that truly caught Adam's eye was a miniature sheet of butterflies.

The butterfly sheet was vibrant and colorful, with each stamp showing a different type of butterfly in stunning detail. Together, the stamps formed a meadow of flowers, with butterflies fluttering around. It was like holding a little piece of nature in his hands.

"I want this one, Dad!" Adam said excitedly. "It's perfect for my collection."

His dad agreed, and they bought the sheet. Back at home, Adam carefully placed the butterfly miniature sheet in a special section of his album. He admired how each butterfly stamp was unique, yet together they created a scene of beauty and tranquility. He decided to write a small description for the sheet: *"Miniature Sheet: Butterflies of the World – A glimpse into the colorful world of butterflies."*

Over the next few weeks, Adam's fascination with miniature sheets grew. He learned that they could be found in all sorts of themes, from animals and plants to famous historical moments and cultural celebrations. Each sheet was like a mini-artwork, and he began to think of ways to build a collection just for miniature sheets.

One day, his dad surprised him with a miniature sheet featuring marine life. The sheet showed different sea creatures like dolphins, turtles, and colorful fish, all forming a picture of an underwater reef. Adam was thrilled and carefully added it to his growing collection.

As he collected more sheets, Adam realized that these miniature sheets were like windows into different worlds. They allowed him to explore diverse topics, each one packed with intricate details and fascinating stories. His album now had a section dedicated to these sheets, with each one labeled and organized by theme.

One evening, as he looked through his album, Adam felt proud. He had stamps that showed individual animals, holiday themes, historical figures, and now, these beautiful miniature sheets. His collection was no longer just about gathering stamps—it was a way to appreciate art, learn about different subjects, and explore the world without leaving home.

"Dad," he said, smiling, "I think miniature sheets are my favorite. They're like having little paintings in my album."

His dad nodded, pleased. "They really are special, Adam. And you're building a collection that's rich in history, nature, and art—all in one place."

Adam felt inspired to keep searching for more miniature sheets, excited for the new themes and worlds they would bring to his collection. With each new sheet he added, he knew he was filling his album with not just stamps, but with tiny, colorful stories from around the world.

Adam's Stamp Exchange Pen Pal

Adam's stamp collection had grown significantly, with stamps from different themes and countries filling his album. But he wanted to expand it even more and find stamps from places he hadn't yet explored. One afternoon, as he browsed a website for young collectors, he came across an idea that thrilled him: joining a pen pal stamp exchange program.

Excited, he turned to his dad. "Dad, I found this program where I can have a pen pal from another country! We would write letters and send each other stamps from our own collections. Do you think I could try it?"

His dad smiled. "That sounds like a fantastic way to learn about other places and add unique stamps to your collection. Let's sign you up and see who your pen pal will be!"

A few weeks later, Adam received a letter from his new pen pal, Luis, who lived in Argentina. Luis introduced himself, saying that he loved football and enjoyed collecting stamps of famous landmarks. Along with the letter, he sent Adam a few stamps from Argentina. One showed a powerful Andean condor soaring over the mountains, another had a picture of the famous Iguazu Falls, and a third featured an old train from the beautiful region of Patagonia.

Adam was thrilled with the stamps and carefully added them to his album. He decided to write back to Luis right away. In his letter, he introduced himself, talked about his love for animals and nature stamps, and included a few stamps from his own collection—a bald eagle from the

United States, a lighthouse on the New England coast, and one of the Statue of Liberty.

As the weeks went by, Adam and Luis exchanged letters regularly. Each letter was a little adventure, packed with stories, questions, and, of course, new stamps. Through their letters, Adam learned about the traditions, holidays, and landscapes of Argentina. Luis shared stories about the Pampas, the wide-open grasslands, and the vibrant festivals held in Buenos Aires. Adam, in turn, told Luis about his life in the U.S., sharing stories about the Grand Canyon, Yellowstone, and even a bit about his stamp-collecting adventures.

One day, Luis sent Adam a very special surprise—a miniature sheet of animals native to Argentina. It featured animals like the puma, the guanaco (a relative of the llama), and the beautiful pink flamingos found in the country's wetlands. Adam was overjoyed and added it to his album with a big note that read: *"From my pen pal Luis in Argentina: Wildlife of Argentina."*

As their friendship grew, Adam realized that he was learning so much more than he ever could have imagined. His collection was no longer just a solo hobby; it had become a way to connect with someone far away, sharing stories, learning about different cultures, and building a friendship that spanned the globe.

One evening, as Adam looked through his album, he felt grateful. He hadn't just added new stamps; he'd added memories, stories, and even a little piece of Luis's world. His album was now filled with not only stamps but with the excitement of exploring and connecting with someone from a different part of the world.

"Dad," Adam said with a smile, "my collection isn't just about stamps anymore. It's like I'm traveling the world and making friends along the way."

His dad nodded, proud of the connections Adam had made. "That's the beauty of collecting, Adam. It's not just about what you gather, but about the connections, friendships, and memories you build along the way."

Adam couldn't agree more. He knew that each new letter from Luis would bring a fresh story and maybe even a new stamp. His pen pal had turned his collection into something even more meaningful—a way to experience the world and share it with someone who shared his passion.

Printed in Great Britain
by Amazon